# DAILY REFLECTIONS
# WITH THE SAINTS

# DAILY REFLECTIONS
# WITH THE SAINTS

### THIRTY INSPIRING REFLECTIONS
### AND CONCLUDING PRAYERS

By

REV. RAWLEY MYERS

*Illustrated*

CATHOLIC BOOK PUBLISHING CO.
New York

NIHIL OBSTAT: James T. O'Connor, S.T.D.
*Censor Librorum*
IMPRIMATUR: ✠ Patrick J. Sheridan, D.D.
*Vicar General, Archdiocese of New York*

(T-880)

1 2 3 4 5 6 7 8 9 10 11 12 13 14 15

# CONTENTS

# INTRODUCTION

THE Saints are our guides in life. Some today chase after every self-anointed guru who comes along. They are often prayerless wonders who soon fade. The Saints, our brothers and sisters in Christ, are our tried and true guides. They were Christ's closest friends; they knew Him better than anyone, so they, better than anyone, can lead us to heaven to be with Christ.

We must not these days be fooled by people who call themselves experts and are listened to because they are bold and articulate. Many of these individuals in religion are in love with novelty and do not know what they are talking about.

Each of us wishes to gain heaven. We cannot follow just anyone who proclaims he knows the way. We know the Saints do know the way.

If you were going on a fishing trip up into the Canadian Rockies, the first thing you would want would be a tried and true guide, not just anyone. For without a good guide, one with experience, you would soon get lost and walk around in circles and perish. The same is true in the spiritual life.

Walking with the Saints, follow their sterling example  and you will reach your cherished goal.

## 1st Day

## ST. BENEDICT

**Patriarch of Western Monasticism**

480-547                                    Feast: July 11

THE monasteries founded by St. Benedict were like lighthouses in the night during the Dark Ages. They civilized and made Christians of the barbarians, who had destroyed what they could not understand, and they could understand almost nothing. The monks taught them to

**7**

farm, to love God, and to respect learning. The monasteries brought back civilization to Europe.

Benedict, a young Roman from a prosperous family, ran away from Rome because, as he said, the schools there were full of "learned ignorance," and he was seeking the "unlearned wisdom" of Jesus.

Benédict at first lived in a cave in a rocky place called Subiaco. But soon other young Christians came to share his life, and so they built huts and began to farm. This was the first monastery in the West.

The Benedictine motto is "Pray and Work." The monks spent their days in chapel and in the fields of the farm. Benedict knew that prayer is essential and work is therapy. So they were men of prayer and labor. Benedict said, "You will truly be monks if you live by the labor of your hands." Work is a rest from prayer and a preparation for prayer. Prayer is all important. No one knows God who does not pray.

Some of the monks became scholars. They had libraries and they worked in scriptoriums, where by hand they copied out books, thereby preserving some of the greatest thoughts of the ancient world. When the books in the cities were destroyed by the barbarians, the monastic libraries saved learning.

Benedict said, "Whatever good work you begin to do, beg of God with most earnest prayer to perfect it." His words are full of common sense and moderation.

Cardinal Newman wrote, "Benedict found the world, physical and social, in ruin, and his mission was to restore it." The barbarians destroyed; Benedict's silent men were builders. When what they built was destroyed, they built again. As Newman stated, "When ill-treated they did not take vengeance, or remember evil, but they gave forth fresh branches of even richer quality."

### Prayer

DEAR St. Benedict, you showed us that the ways of the world are foolish. We must pray and grow in friendship with Jesus. Please embrace us and help us in our needs.

Look after the sick in body and the sick in soul in our world. Help us to tell them of Jesus. Many are waiting. Who will feed them? Obtain for us hearts of love to work for Jesus and bring souls to Him. Amen.

# 2nd Day

# ST. BRIGID

## Second Patron of Ireland

450-525                                    Feast: February 1

WHEN Brigid was a little girl, St. Patrick converted the Irish. She was brought up near Kildare—a beautiful and attractive high-born, high-spirited young lady. Her father was Duffy, a pagan chieftain; her mother was a Christian slave. Despite her family's attempt to have her marry, she insisted on being a nun. She refused her many suitors and became a bride of Christ.

Brigid was the first of countless Irish Sisters to serve Jesus. As was written, "God gave His graces to her." Because she prayed frequently and fervently, she was blessed by Jesus and His love filled her heart.

Her father strongly and stubbornly opposed her notions, and so Brigid slipped away from her home and presented herself to the bishop. Other young women joined her and the bishop said, "You shall be called Sisters of Mercy." They prayed and did penance and, with mercy, went out to help the helpless.

All her life Brigid saw Christ in people in need. As an Irish historian records, "Brigid always arrived at a place when she was most needed." Her heart was on fire with love for Christ, and like Christ she loved the needy.

Often she sold everything and gave the money to the poor. And in the convent, though she was the superior, she did all the ordinary work: cleaning, scrubbing on her knees, sweeping, and tending the chickens and the cows.

Brigid founded other convents, schools, and hospitals. Prayer was her great spiritual strength. She never allowed herself to be too busy–even in good works—to pray. Prayer gave Brigid the courage to do Christ's work in the world. She was not like some today who neglect prayer and become discouraged in their work for Christ. Because of prayer, she knew that friendship with Jesus is all important, and friendship comes from visiting with Him. Without real friendship with Jesus, a person can do nothing worthwhile.

She was often found before the Tabernacle, in silence, talking to Jesus, away from the noise and busyness of the world. There she spoke to Him and He spoke to her.

When Brigid died all Ireland mourned her, for all Ireland loved her. Because of her ceaseless work for Christ, the chronicler said, "Ireland would never be quite the same without Brigid."

### Prayer

DEAR St. Brigid, you gave your life to Jesus. Help us to love Him more. Pray that we may have more Christlike hearts so that we will reach out, as you did, and help others, touching them with Christ's love.

Help us to bring His message of goodness to the confused. Those who spread His love, He loves the most. Let kindness guide our lives. Jesus wishes, not more talk, but more deeds of kindness. Assist us in showing His love. Amen.

## 3rd Day
# ST. CATHERINE LABOURÉ

**Instrument of Mary Immaculate**

1806-1876　　　　　　　Feast: November 25

CATHERINE'S father refused to let her go to the convent. To get this idea out of her mind, he sent her off from their village to visit her brother in Paris. She worked for a time as a waitress in her brother's cafe.

However, some of the laboring men who ate there flirted with her, embarrassing this young country girl. Because of this, Zoe, her name before becoming a Sister, was sent to visit another brother whose wife had a school for girls. Here the snobbish pupils looked down on her.

To get away from this torment Zoe went to visit a nearby convent. She trembled as she walked along, asking herself, "I wonder if this is what God wants me to be?" When she arrived at the convent, she was shown into the parlor. She looked around—and stopped short! Her eyes were fixed on a large picture that hung on the wall. She asked the Sister, "Who is that priest?" The nun replied, "Why that is our father founder, St. Vincent de Paul."

Zoe gasped, for as a young woman back in her village, she had had a curious dream of an old priest offering Mass in their parish church. She didn't know who he was, only that his face was kindly. After Mass he motioned to her to come. She was frightened and left the church. Then, in her dream, she went to visit a sick friend.

When she entered the house of her friend, there was the same old priest again, and he said to her, "My child, it is a good thing to care for the sick. You draw away from me, but the day will come when you will be glad to come to me." Zoe left the house very happy, and then she woke up. Now, looking at this picture of St. Vincent, she was certain he had called her to be a Sister here.

She wrote her father. It was beyond belief that he gave permission and she became a Sister of Charity of St. Vincent de Paul. Because she was unlearned she was the kitchen Sister: washing dishes, cooking, doing the laundry, and feeding the chickens. But she was fervent in prayer.

Sister Catherine said, "Here I am, Blessed Mother. I have nothing to offer God except myself, but that I offer with all my heart." And the Blessed Mother appeared to this humble Saint and gave her the Miraculous Medal. Through this medal countless blessings have been received by followers of Mary throughout the world.

### Prayer

D EAR St. Catherine, you were the lowest member of the convent, yet Mary appeared to you. You teach us that humility is the way to God. God's ways are holy, and holy is the way of life that leads to Him.

Holy is the way from captivity to freedom; holy is the joy He gives us; holy are the trials we endure. Holy are families that follow our Lord. And holy is death with Jesus at our side. Humility is the secret to holiness. Help us to be humble. Amen.

# 4th Day

# ST. COLUMBAN

## Indefatigable Missionary

540-615 Feast: November 23

THE influence of this outstanding Irish missionary on the continent of Europe was very great. His foundation of a monastery in France was the nursery of bishops, and, as one contemporary commentator wrote, "He hurled the fire of Christ wherever he went." The Holy Father, Pope Pius XI, in our own century said, "The renaissance of Christian learning in France, Germany, and Italy is due to the work and zeal of St. Columban."

In the days of St. Columban, Ireland was "at the edge of the world," but here the Faith burned brightly and the zeal of her missionaries was tremendous.

Columban was a handsome, healthy youth with a keen mind. His attractive personality, insightful intelligence, and deep spirituality led him to become a monk and a well known preacher.

Columban became a missionary, and he and his companions went to France and founded there a monastery. After the destruction of the barbarians, there was much work to do for Christ. Slaughter and war were everywhere. Lust, jealousy, and murder prevailed. These wild uncivilized warriors were more like animals than men.

But many heeded the preaching of Columban. He told them, "Understand created things, if you want to know the Creator." Regarding penance he said, "Humility makes you strong; self-denial makes you Christlike." And he warned, "Let us concern ourselves with heavenly things; like pilgrims always sigh for our homeland of heaven." And Columban founded many monasteries.

Columban's sermons, however, disturbed the egotistical king. And the missionary was sent into exile. The days were difficult, for he and his companions were often hungry and always cold, but he said, "How wonderful are God's ways, letting us be in want, so that He can show us His love in coming to our aid; allowing us to be tempted so that we will draw closer to Him."

The Saint added, "The true disciple of Christ Crucified should follow Him with the Cross. That person is blessed who shares in His Passion and shame." He stated, "If we suffer with Jesus, we shall also reign with Him."

Columban exhorted, "Let us pray that God will wound our hearts with His love, that the Lord will light the flame of His goodness in us." He prayed always that his own lamp would give light to others.

Columban died in a monastery he established in the mountains of northern Italy.

### Prayer

ST. Columban, you spread the Word of Jesus far and wide. Help us to do the same. Like you, may our ways be holy as we journey through life. We look to Jesus and know that we are safe with our hand in His.

Let us walk side by side with Jesus so that we will reach the Promised Land of heaven where we will be happy with Him, our families, and all our loved ones forever and ever. Amen.

# 5th Day

## ST. EDMUND CAMPION

### One of the Forty English Martyrs

1540-1581                    Feast: October 25

EDMUND attracted notice at Oxford as a young student when he made a speech to welcome Queen Elizabeth. He so pleased her that he came to be called "one of the diamonds of England." He seemed destined to be a bishop in the Church of England. But then he left Oxford and England and went to the Catholic University in Belgium. For his scholarship had convinced him that he could no longer in conscience give allegiance to Elizabeth's Church. In Europe, he studied to be a Jesuit priest.

In time, Campion was sent back to England, to bring the Sacraments and the Mass to the Catholics hiding there. To be a Catholic under Queen Elizabeth was to be put in prison or killed.

Campion managed to stay in the Catholic underground for many months. He had entered England in disguise and often hid in attics, barns, and basements. In various disguises, he went about hearing Confessions, baptizing, and offering the Holy

Mass. He wrote to Rome, "The harvest is wonderful and great."

Edmund was a learned scholar, and he wrote a pamphlet that proved that the Catholic Church was the ancient Christian Church that went back to the time of the Apostles, showing that Elizabeth's Church of England was man-made. This, of course, made the queen furious, and her soldiers redoubled their efforts to capture him.

The holy priest should have curtailed his activities, but so many Catholics secretly begged for the Mass that he could not refuse them, even though every new contact was dangerous. There were spies everywhere.

Edmund's travels at times took him by Tyburn where Catholics were put to death for their Faith. Each time he prayed because he knew it would someday be the place of his death.

One day, after offering Mass at a Catholic estate, Edmund was having dinner with the family. Suddenly there were soldiers outside. A spy, pretending to be a Catholic, had come to the house and learned that the great Father Campion was there and brought the soldiers. There was a large reward for finding the Jesuit.

The Catholics hid Campion, and after two searches, the soldiers could not find him. They stayed the night, and when they were about to leave, one official saw a light from a crack in the wall. The panel was chopped open, and Campion was found. He was taken to London and executed at Tyburn.

### Prayer

DEAR St. Edmund, you gave your life for Jesus. May we live for Him. God has laid His hand on us and has called us by name. Keep us close to Him, the source of all joy. Jesus came into the world to save us. Help us to walk in His ways.

Christ is light for our darkness, joy for our sadness, bread to nourish us, our life to overcome death. Obtain for us the grace to sing His glory. Amen.

# 6th Day

# BL. KATERI TEKAKWITHA

## Lily of the Mohawks

1656-1680                                    Feast: July 14

THE Mohawk Indians raided the Algonquin village, killing many and taking a host of prisoners. They brought the captives back to camp to torture them. Just as one beautiful Algonquin girl was about to be beaten and clubbed as she ran through the path of the torture, the Mohawk chief pulled her aside. He gave her to his sister to be her slave.

The girl's name was Kahenta. She was a Christian. When she grew up, the chief took her for his wife. To them was born Tekakwitha, the Lily of the Mohawks.

Some time later, there was gloom and despair among the Mohawks. The "smallpox devil" had taken many lives. The chief himself lay dying. His wife and young son were already dead. His little daughter Tekakwitha was seriously ill.

The chief died; the daughter survived. Her eyes were weakened and her pretty face was scarred for life. She was a quiet girl who remembered the beautiful stories her mother had told her about Jesus, Who suffered so that human beings could go to heaven, and His lovely Mother, who was a Virgin.

Tekakwitha's mother had taught her how to pray to Jesus, and when she was alone she loved to do so. But her aunt was now in charge, and she was mean and always complained, because Tekakwitha, with her poor eyesight, was slow in her work. The aunt was constantly scolding and complaining about the girl, who merely bowed her head and continued with her duties.

In time the French forced the Mohawks to allow the blackrobes, the Jesuit missionaries, to come to their village. Tekakwitha's heart jumped for joy when she heard this. But her aunt forbade her to talk to the priests. She could only dream of one day receiving the "Saving Waters."

One day Kateri slipped away with a companion, hiding in the forest, moving north at night. They wished to go to the Christian village where they would be safe. A search party sought them, but God protected them. They traveled a long distance; at length they came to the village of Christians.

"Now I can live close to Christ," Kateri said.

Kateri was so devout in prayer that all looked upon her as a Saint. She became very ill and soon died. Before dying she said, "I will love you in heaven and help you."

### Prayer

DEAR Blessed Kateri, you were known for many sacrifices for Christ. You suffered great hardships to know and love Him. Pray for us.

God holds us in the palm of His hand. Like you, may we always be faithful to Him and thank Him for life and love, for knowledge and strength, for bread and shelter, for faith and hope. Pray for us and our loved ones every day. Amen.

# 7th Day

# ST. LAURENCE O'TOOLE

## Archbishop of Dublin

1128-1180                          Feast: November 14

OF noble birth, Laurence was a descendant of local kings in Leinster. He became an Augustinian canon and at the age of twenty-five Abbot of Glendalough Abbey. Later the clergy and people of Dublin elected him as their spiritual leader, their archbishop.

During the difficult days of the Norman attacks on the city, Laurence suffered the siege with the people and was instrumental in eventually negotiating a treaty.

When Laurence was only ten, in a battle fought by his father, he was taken hostage by the enemy. For two years he toiled as a slave, until he was able to escape.

As an abbot, he used all the resources of the monastery to aid the hungry when famine struck. As Dublin's bishop, he was popular with the people, but not with many of the clergy whom he tried to reform. He demanded they do penance, and he gave the example.

In fact, Laurence did much more than any of his clergy; under his rich episcopal garments he wore a hairshirt. On Fridays, he ate only bread and water. At night, after a weary day with the people, he prayed for long periods.

This tall, handsome prelate instructed the children himself, visited the sick, and begged for the poor.

When the Earl of Pembroke, nicknamed "Strongbow," invaded Ireland and advanced on Dublin, the archbishop courageously met the enemy army and tried to dissuade them from fighting. In this he failed. During the battle he spent his days tending the wounded and protecting the innocent from massacre.

St. Laurence prayed constantly; he knew that in going to Jesus we give up nothing and gain everything. Far from taking anything from us except our selfishness, Christ wants to give us His love, His blessings, His help. He wants to exchange the anxiety in our hearts for peace of soul, the greatest gift of all. Laurence learned early, on his knees, that Jesus gives us the robe of glory and happiness of heart.

When Laurence was dying someone asked him about making a will. He smiled and said, "God knows I have not a penny in the world."

## Prayer

**D**EAR St. Laurence, you cared for the people. There are many today who are afflicted. Help us to assist sick souls, lift up the needy, fill the hungry, strengthen the feeble, and give courage to the discouraged.

Please pray that we may have spiritual strength and faith like yours, so that we may aid others. Bless those who are near and dear to us. May Jesus take care of them always. Amen.

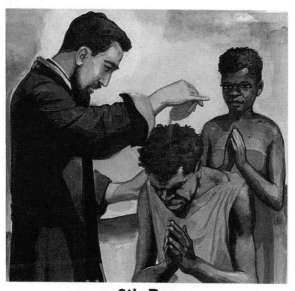

## 8th Day
# ST. PETER CLAVER
### Apostle to Slaves

1581-1654                    Feast: September 9

PETER was a Spanish Jesuit who gave himself to the service and the salvation of the slaves in the Caribbean islands. For more than forty years he labored tirelessly for these wretched people, most often treated like animals rather than humans. He called himself "the slave of the slaves." He was their apostle, father, physician, and friend. He fed them, nursed them with tenderness, and took care of their loathsome diseases. He worked to ease their oppression and to soften the hearts of their masters.

Whenever Peter heard of a new slave ship coming into the harbor, he was there comforting the frightened, crushed, forlorn souls. He was, of course, bitterly criticized by the slave owners. They put many difficulties in his way. His reply was simply, "The humble ass is my model. When he is evilly spoken of, he is dumb. Whatever happens he never complains, for he is only an ass. So also must God's servants be."

As a young man, Peter graduated with distinction from the Jesuit College in Barcelona. He joined the Society of Jesus and was assigned to teach at the new Jesuit College on the Mediterranean island of Majorca, off the coast of Spain.

There, Peter, a gifted professor, was most impressed by the old assistant gatekeeper, a Jesuit Brother named Alonso Rodriguez. Alonso, in the lowest place in the college, was the most saintly. Though Alonso was ignored by most of the self-centered professors, Peter found him to be a gentle man of great wisdom. He was full of childlike faith and Christlike love. Peter learned more from the unlearned Brother than from the faculty of the prestigious college.

Brother Alonso encouraged Peter to go as a missionary to the New World "where the harvest is abundant, but there are few workers." He said, "Many souls in America might be saved by a zealous missionary. The pagans there are like unpolished diamonds who can be brightened into things of beauty." He added, "If the glory of God's house concerns you, go to the West Indies and save those perishing souls."

And so Peter went. He landed at Cartagena, an important Spanish island in the Caribbean. He saw the awful condition of the slaves and served them the rest of his life.

### Prayer

DEAR St. Peter, you helped the poorest of the poor. You assisted the poor slaves while others ridiculed you. You neglected yourself to help the neglected.

You imitated Jesus, Who suffered even more for us. Taken prisoner to set us free, He kept silent while people humiliated Him. Crowned with thorns to make us kings, He died on the Cross to give us life. O St. Peter, help us to be more grateful. Amen.

## 9th Day
## ST. PHILIP NERI

**Model of Cheerful Holiness**

1515-1594                    Feast: May 26

PHILIP was born in Florence but as a youth went to Rome. A devout soul, he sometimes spent the whole night in prayer in the catacombs. He worked with other young men and formed a little group to help the sick and poor.

In prayer, Philip felt himself infused with the love of God, and he wanted to share

this love with others. His appealing personality won friends and followers from all
walks of life, from beggars to cardinals.

When Philip was thirty-six, at the urging
of his confessor he became a priest, but his
work in Rome remained largely the same.
He arranged talks, had discussion groups
and prayer circles, and became an out-
standing confessor and spiritual director,
often piercing the pride and pretenses of
the penitent with his splendid humor.
Sometimes, he took the young people on
excursions to visit other churches in Rome,
with music and a picnic on the way.

In time some of his disciples became
priests and joined him. They called their
house the Oratory, a place of prayer.

At first, as a priest, Philip had only a few
followers; they came to his room. But the
number grew and became so large they
had to have a hall. After silent prayer and
spiritual reading, Philip would speak to
them. And they had beautiful spiritual
music as a part of their program.

Philip was known and loved throughout
Rome, from the Holy Father to street boys.
He counseled popes, cardinals and many oth-
ers. He constantly refused honors for himself.

Philip knew pride was the root of evil
and he frequently deflated pompous peo-

ple. Even more, he disliked cheerless, gloomy, puritanical people. He felt that if Christ's followers could not be happy, then who in the wide world could be? We are Easter people, disciples of the Risen Christ, full of hope and happiness. At the Oratory he told the young men who came, "I will have no sadness in this house. Don't be forever dwelling on your sins—leave a little for the Angels to do."

Philip was accused by some of being heretical and his work suffered from gossip mongers, but the Holy Father backed him and encouraged him.

Philip's whole earthly existence was a joyful journey, for he put all things in the hands of God, trusting Him completely. He prayed, "Let me get through today, and I shall not fear tomorrow."

### Prayer

YOU were a clown for Christ, dear St. Philip. You were always happy and smiling. You wanted no gloomy faces in your house. You were so joyful because you put all things in the hands of God. You trusted Him completely. You knew that He would take care of you always.

Help us to do the same. Ask Jesus to give us a happy heart and more faith so that we don't worry all the time. Amen.

# 10th Day

# ST. ROBERT SOUTHWELL

### Priest-Poet and Martyr

1561-1595                      Feast: October 25

LIKE Edmund Campion, Robert was a Jesuit priest who returned in disguise to England during the days when Catholics were persecuted by the Crown. He offered Mass many times in hiding. The Catholics so loved the Mass that they pleaded for it whenever they could find a priest. Like Campion, Robert was captured by the officials, imprisoned, and put to death for his Faith at Tyburn.

Robert Southwell wrote beautiful poetry:

My soul, with Christ join thou in fight;
Stick to the tents that he hath plight;
With his crib is surest ward,
This little Babe will be thy guard;
If thou wilt foil thy foes with joy,
Then flee not from the heavenly Boy.

Here Robert is telling us the Child of Bethlehem will always protect us if we stay close to Him. He gives us strength, courage and joy, and peace.

With his eyes on Christ he wrote:

O dying souls, behold your living
     spring;
O dazzled eyes, behold your sun of
     grace;
Dull ears, attend what word this Word
     doth bring;
Up, heavy hearts, with joy your Joy em-
     brace.
From death, from dark, from deafness,
     from despairs,
This life, this light, this Word this joy
     repairs.

Robert wrote this moving meditation on
death:

Before my face the picture hangs,
That daily should put me in mind
Of those cold qualms and bitter pangs,
That shortly I am like to find:
But yet, alas, full little I
Do think hereon, that I must die.
If none can 'scape death's dreadful
     dart,
If rich and poor his beck obey,
If strong, if wise, if all do smart,
Then I to 'scape shall have no way.
Oh! grant me grace, O God, that I
My life may mend, since I must die!

### Prayer

D EAR St. Robert, not even the worst kind of prison conditions could deter you from writing inspiring poetry. Help us to see the beauty in the world and not always be thinking about the evil here. Ask Jesus to watch over us and give us light so that we may be filled with hope rather than pessimism.

Pray that our Lord may be at our side and always protect us. Obtain for us the grace to serve Christ with joy and humility, please Him with our kindness to others, and await His Coming with hope. Amen.

# 11th Day

# ST. THOMAS BECKET

## Outstanding Bishop and Martyr

1118-1170                    Feast: December 29

AS a young man, Thomas was a favorite of King Henry II of England. In fact, the monarch appointed him his Chancellor of the Realm. He was a constant companion of the king at wild parties and always dressed in splendid attire. Then the Archbishop of Canterbury died. Henry decided that his best friend, Thomas, should be named archbishop.

When the king told him, Thomas exclaimed, "No. Do not do this to me." King Henry asked why. "You are my closest friend, and you will see to it that the Church obeys the king." Thomas pleaded to be spared this position, but, as always, King Henry had his way.

Thomas, as archbishop, completely changed. As a youth with Henry, he loved "wine, women, and song." But now he was not the same person at all, always praying and doing penance. He discarded the glamor and glitter of the court. And soon he was defending the rights of the Church against the king even more than the old archbishop had done.

Henry was beside himself with rage. He felt his friend had betrayed him. He rued the day he made Thomas the archbishop. Like a spoiled child, as most kings were, Henry wanted to run everything in England, including the Church.

Their differences became so pronounced that Thomas was forced to go into exile, fleeing to France. He lived there in a monastery. At length a truce was reached, and Thomas returned to Canterbury. But they began to argue again. King Henry in disgust and frustration cried out one day, "Is there no one to rid me of this troublesome prelate?"

Four of his knights took him at his word. Shortly after Christmas, they went to the Cathedral at Canterbury. They threatened Thomas, but he quietly replied, "It will be easy to take care of me, for I will not run away."

The next day they rushed at him as he was going to the altar. He could have escaped, but he would not. Undefended and helpless, he simply stood there. They hacked him up with their swords.

Thomas, as archbishop, would not be the pawn of the king and let him run roughshod over the Church. True, as a youth, they were cronies and companions in wild parties, but Thomas matured and the king did not. As archbishop, Thomas knew he was responsible for the Church and would not bend when the king unjustly wished to use it for his own worldly purposes. It was then that the long duel began that ended in the death of Thomas, a martyr for the Faith.

### Prayer

D EAR St. Thomas, you gave your life for Christ, yet we are so childish, proud, jealous, and anxious. Pray for us that we may overcome our weakness and grow in faith, hope, and kindness.

Ask Jesus to lead us on the way and remain with us as the night comes on. Obtain strength of soul for us in the storms of life. Teach us that we need God's grace because of ourselves we can do nothing. Amen.

# 12th Day
# ST. JOHN DE BRÉBEUF
## One of the North American Martyrs

1596-1649                    Feast: October 19

JOHN was a Jesuit missionary, a black-robe, to the Indians in North America. He was born in Normandy in northern France. His parents and grandparents had lived there during terrible religious wars and had remained staunch Catholics. When John was sixteen, tall and well built, he went to the nearby Jesuit school; it was there that he decided to enter the Society of Jesus.

Open, clear-eyed, and unafraid of work, John was an excellent candidate. But toward the end of his long seminary years, he suddenly became very ill with tuberculosis, and his huge frame shrunk so that he looked like a skeleton. He was weakening so fast, that his superiors decided to ordain him early, because they were sure he would soon die.

But after his ordination, the young priest gradually began to improve. He gave himself over to prayer, and he regained his health—so much so that when, later, the Jesuits opened a mission in New France (Canada), he sent in his name. He was certain he would be refused because of his health, but still he prayed to go. One day he was handed a sealed envelope. When he opened it he could not believe it. He had been chosen to be a missionary!

Now, it was twenty-five years since he first started work for Christ among the Huron Indians. He had suffered untold hardship. His beard and hair were grisly gray. It was a peaceful day and he was visiting a village, when suddenly shrieks filled the air. The mortal enemies of the Hurons, the Iroquois, came charging out of the forest. They overran everything, killed all who resisted them, and took the others prisoners.

John was one of the captives. The Iroquois danced around him. They stripped the priest and the others and forced their captives to run through their lines, brutally beating them. At the end of this horrible ordeal, the priest huddled among the Hurons and prayed for his captors.

Then the Iroquois chose the blackrobe, "the white-skinned giant" and made him run up and down. They hit him and leaped on him and broke his bones and chewed his fingers. They dragged him to a torture post, tied him to it, and drove a spear into his heart.

### Prayer

O NOBLE martyr, St. John, how brave and faithful you were. Help us, we pray. Ask God to make us brave and loyal to Him always. In our youth, He saw us through turbulent times; in our adulthood, He instructs us about life and love and helps us pray.

Impress on our minds our great need for God in everything we do. Teach us to be ever grateful for all God's gifts, for you know better than we do that we must continue to have His graces in order to walk in goodness. Amen.

## 13th Day
## ST. MONICA

**Exemplary Mother and Widow**

332-387                    Feast: August 27

MONICA was the mother of the great St. Augustine. She was a Christian, but her husband was a pagan and an unprincipled libertine. Monica prayed endlessly for her brilliant, wayward son, but he followed his father and was even encouraged by him to live for pleasure.

Monica worried all the while for Augustine was vain and sensual. The lad, proud and passionate, went from bad to worse. As a teen he was reckless, unreliable, and selfish. When Monica tried to admonish him, he brushed her words off as the chatter of a woman. He was a man—praying and religion were for weak women. To make matters worse, his father bragged about the boy's sexual exploits.

Monica had to stand by and watch and could do nothing. Confusion and violence reigned  in the town where they lived in North Africa. She pleaded in prayer for God's help for her son. Yet the dominant father badly trained the boy. He was too lenient with him when he was in a good mood and too severe with him when in a fit of anger.

The lad did wrong for the sheer excitement of doing evil. Sex confusedly boiled over in him. He resigned  himself wholly to his passions and then found himself their slave. He wrote later, "My God, my Mercy, how much gall did You mingle into my lustfulness. I secretly entered the prison of pleasure and was sorrowfully bound with its chains."

Monica would weep when she saw this. She prayed endlessly for her son, but it did not seem to help. In fact, things got worse. When Augustine was seventeen, he went away from home to school in Carthage, a much more wicked city than their town.

Monica at times must have been near despair, and yet she continued to pray for her sinful son. In her grief, she went weeping to the bishop for advice. The man of God told her, "Go now and God bless you. It is not possible that the son of so many tears should be lost."

Yet after all her fervent prayers, a still more severe blow fell. Augustine announced that he was leaving Africa for Rome, which then was the "cesspool of iniquity."

Still she prayed and it was in Rome that Augustine began to think deep thoughts. He failed there and went to Milan, and it was there that he met the great Bishop St. Ambrose. And in Milan Augustine turned to Christ with his whole heart, and all of Monica's prayers were answered.

### Prayer

DEAR St. Monica, holy mother, teach us how to persevere in prayer as you did for your son, Augustine. Ask God to bless our parents who taught us and prayed for us and our teachers who were our guides in youth.

Help us to be more thankful to God, for we are forgetful. We dislike ingratitude in others; do not let us be ungrateful. Amen.

# 14th Day
# ST. ROSE PHILIPPINE DUCHESNE
## Missionary Teacher

1769-1852                           Feast: November 18

ALL her life, Rose Duchesne wanted to be a missionary to the Indians in America. She lived in France and entered the convent much against her parents' wishes. Then the convent was closed and the sisters were exiled, during the horrible days of destruction and bloodshed following the French Revolution.

Even then, as a young laywoman, Rose started an orphanage for the many children left without parents. And in time she was able to recover the convent. Her wealthy father leased it. She and a few pious women moved the orphanage there and formed a pious society.

At length, they became a part of the Society of the Sacred Heart, a new French community of nuns headed by Mother Madeleine Sophie Barat. Mother Barat, now also a Saint, came herself to give Rose Philippine and her companions a year of special spiritual training. When the two Saints met, they were friends at once, being of one mind. Rose, the founder of the small group, most gladly gave up her leadership position and became a humble novice, the most humble and prayerful of all.

Then Rose, now a nun known as Mother Duchesne, was named secretary to Mother Barat at the motherhouse in Paris. It seemed that her dreams of being a missionary to the Indians would never come true. One day, however, a missionary bishop from New Orleans-St Louis came to the convent. Mother Duchesne rushed to Mother Barat and said that God had sent him to them.

Mother Barat indicated that if he asked for Sisters she would send them. He did not, however; he only asked if he might celebrate Mass there. Mother Duchesne that evening went to the chapel and prayed as only she could pray. The next morning after Mass the bishop asked for Sisters— and Mother Barat said yes.

In America the Sisters, led by Mother Duchesne, almost starved the first year, giving their food to the poor children who came to their school. They suffered many terrible hardships, but their work prospered and they soon had numerous schools in towns along the Mississippi River.

When Mother Duchesne was very old, the Sisters accepted an Indian mission in Kansas. She went there with the other nuns. She could no longer teach, but she spent almost all day every day in the little log cabin chapel, and she impressed the Indians more than the others. They called her the Woman-Who-Always-Prays.

### Prayer

DEAR St. Rose, how you prayed, and how you suffered to bring Christ to the children! Help us to pray for the children of today, many of whom do not know Jesus and are lost in the jungle of life. On all sides, they are urged to do drugs, to drink and drive, and to have sex before marriage. They need Jesus.

Enable us to pray for them daily and do all we can, as you did, to help them know Christ and love Him. Amen.

## 15th Day
## ST. MADELEINE SOPHIE BARAT

**Virgin and Foundress**

1779-1865                    Feast: May 25

MADELEINE Sophie Barat longed to become a Carmelite Sister and to lose herself in humble service. But she had a keen intellect, and her brother insisted she be highly educated, something rare in her day for a woman. But this was all in God's plan, for at the age of twenty, she was the instrument through which the great Society of the Sacred Heart was founded in Paris.

While she was studying, her brother told her one day that a visitor was coming that afternoon. It was a priest, Father Joseph Varin. He became a regular visitor.

One day the priest said to Sophie, "God has given you a great gift of intelligence. You would make a very good teacher." He wanted to found a Sisterhood of the Society of the Sacred Heart in France. He knew Sophie wished to be a Sister. He now said something to her that took her breath away, "I want you to be the cornerstone of it, Sophie."

And so it came to pass. At first there were only four, but they were humble and prayerful and their numbers grew. At first they had one small school, but soon many.

Sophie was the superior. Her health had never been robust, but she found her strength in prayer. Then one day Father Varin told Mother Barat that he had received a letter from a young woman and her companions in the south of France. The woman's name was Rose Philippine Duchesne. They wanted to become Sisters of the Sacred Heart.

Mother Barat made the long journey there and directed them. Being a Saint, she knew well the ways of the Lord. Was not Jesus her closest Friend?

In time Rose Philippine told Mother of the secret desire to be a missionary to the Indians. Instead of laughing at her as others had done, Mother said she too had had that dream. The two were attuned in heart, loving Christ above all things as they did.

Mother Barat knew she could never fulfill her dream. She was always sacrificing her wants for the good of others, and now for the community. All her life she was the servant of the others as their Mother. Her trials were many, but her trust in God was greater. Her many sacrifices made the Society grow and flourish in many places.

### Prayer

D EAR Mother Barat, you loved children and dedicated your life to seeing that they knew Jesus. We, at times, neglect the children, for we are lulled into complacency by television and many other distractions.

Help us, Mother, to remember to put first things first. The children, first of all, must be taught about Christ. Obtain for us the grace to pass on the Faith to the coming generations. Amen.

## 16th Day
## ST. ISAAC JOGUES

**Apostle to the Indians**

1607-1646                    Feast: October 19

ISAAC was tortured by Iroquois Indians and then forced to be their slave. A missionary to the Indians, Father Isaac, like his fellow Jesuit, Father John de Brébeuf, endured untold hardships to bring Christ to them.

Like John, Isaac was serving the Hurons when captured by the Iroquois. He and the others were taken the full length of Lake Champlain (now in New York State) as prisoners. The voyage was a nightmare of hunger, heat, and festering wounds.

At the Iroquois village, the prisoners had to run through a line while being beaten with clubs and whips. Next, the priest's fingers were crushed. Isaac was then stripped of his clothing and beaten, hacked, and clubbed. Yet, after each ordeal, he prayed with all his heart.

After days of torture, Father Isaac was made a slave. His circumstances were most pitiable; he was forced to work in wretched conditions. He said, "I found my consolation in reading the Bible."

Following many months of intense suffering, the priest was able to escape. He was taken on a Dutch ship from New Amsterdam. Isaac returned to the seminary in France where he had been a student for so long. The priest on the faculty who opened the door did not recognize him because he had been so mutilated.

Despite all this, Father Isaac begged to go back to the Indians. At last he was given permission. Now the Iroquois were peaceful. Isaac went to be their priest for he knew their language.

Eventually, the Bear clan, which believed that the blackrobe was a sorcerer, blamed him for an outbreak of sickness and the failure of their crops. Accordingly, he was seized, tortured, and beheaded.

### Prayer

O ST. Isaac, valiant priest, pray for our priests today. They need the special strength that you had. They need many graces in these difficult days. Let us daily remember priests in our prayers.

Beg Jesus to protect, guide, and direct priests, so that they will walk with Him, for a priest must remain close to Christ. Assist us in our duty to pray for them who help us so much. Amen.

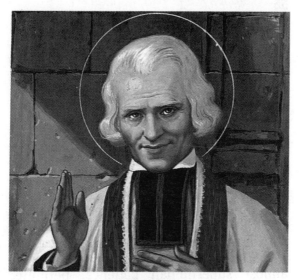

## 17th Day
## ST. JOHN VIANNEY
**Patron of Parish Priests**

1786-1859                    Feast: August 4

JOHN Vianney was born in France. He had a difficult time trying to master book learning. But what he lacked in knowledge, he made up for in wisdom, which came from his constant prayers.

John was from a large and poor family. As he grew up, anticlericalism was rampant following the French Revolution. Many priests were killed or deported. The

Vianneys, devout Catholics, went to distant farmhouses where priests in disguise offered secret Masses for the faithful. They risked their lives to bring the Sacraments to the people. Priests were looked upon as real heroes by John.

At length, Napoleon restored peace for the Church. John worked on his father's small farm until he was nineteen. But he wanted to be a priest, and so a local assistant pastor tutored him in Latin in a class where most of the boys were half his age. While they learned easily, he struggled with every word. He felt like a dunce, but he persevered. And the priest teacher, with almost superhuman patience, permitted him to continue in the class.

When John was twenty-five he went to the seminary. There he was last in a class of two hundred and was mocked by other students. In fact, he did so badly that he was dismissed. But the priest at home began again to tutor him privately in theology. And he persuaded the seminary superior to test John in French instead of Latin. The young student did better, and the bishop, because of John's evident piety, ordained him.

For a time, John was an assistant in the parish of his tutor, and then he was given the parish in the small village of Ars. He became the Cure of Ars. Only a few people there went regularly to church.

But John's prayerfulness and penances changed everything. He prayed and did great penances for the souls of his parishioners. He gave his mattress to a beggar and slept on the floor. And he ate little. Such sanctity is irresistible. People started to come to Mass—not only people from his village but from others and, in time, from all over France.

John spent countless hours hearing Confessions; he never tired of absolving sinners. People flocked to him because here was someone who practiced what he preached.

### Prayer

DEAR St. John, Patron of parish priests, bless our parish priests today and always. May they have the special strength they need to bring Christ to the people. May they have light to know the way, and courage to follow in the footsteps of Jesus.

Beg God to grant His priests plentiful blessings, for they cannot be good priests without them. Today in our semi-pagan world so many influences seek to take them away from Jesus. Help our priests to know that they are tallest when on their knees. Amen.

## 18th Day
## ST. MAXIMILIAN KOLBE

**Apostle of the Printed Word and Martyr**

1894-1941                          Feast: August 14

THIS Polish Franciscan Father lived in our own times. He wanted only to save souls. To this end, he dedicated all his efforts to the Blessed Mother.

Maximilian ended his days in a hell-like Nazi concentration camp, where subhuman guards tried to dehumanize the prisoners. And he stepped forward at the end to give his life for a man with a family who was condemned to die. Even the Nazi officer was amazed saying, "We have never seen the likes of this before."

Maximilian's death was amazing, but so was his life. In an age of apathy, he had great zeal. He wished to feed souls. Father Maximilian was not much to look at; he was frail and slightly stooped, but his soul was golden. He was a man of action, new ideas, and enthusiasm—all for Christ. He took to heart Christ's final command, "Go out and tell everyone about Me." He did indeed hear loud and clear the words of Jesus to shout the Good News from the housetops.

How could he, a simple Franciscan priest, do this? Because he was a Saint, he found a way. He could visit the homes of many with a small publication. He started with a newsletter. Everything seemed against him. His superior was not enthusiastic and he himself was not in good health. But he prayed to the Mother of All Grace to help him. The project began, though the superior said the house had no money to give him. "You must raise the money," he said.

For love of Mary, Maximilian began to beg, but he hated every minute of it. He started out going from house to house in the area, confused and embarrassed. It was so painful for him. Before he got up enough nerve to knock at the first door, he turned back three times. Finally, he said a prayer to our Lady and got the strength to beg. He received enough funds to get started.

From that most humble beginning, Maximilian went on to put out a magazine that eventually reached hundreds of thousands in Poland and in many other parts of the world. The message of Jesus was being read by millions!

This simple Franciscan Father showed what prayer can do.

One day a bishop came by and looked at the large printing plant and said, "What would St. Francis do if he saw all these expensive machines?"

Father Maximilian answered, "He would roll up his sleeves and start to work with us."

### Prayer

DEAR St. Maximilian, humble Franciscan, great Apostle of the press, heroic martyr in the concentration camp, please help us. Pray for us. You know full well how much we need God's grace.

Enable us to imitate you in spreading the message of Jesus in a world where most people forget Him or ignore Him. Pray that we may have your zeal to tell others about how much Jesus loves us. Amen.

# ST. MARGARET OF SCOTLAND

### Christian Queen and Model Widow

1050-1093                    Feast: November 16

MARGARET was a beautiful young princess, born in Hungary, the daughter of Edward, an English prince-in-exile, and Agatha, a princess-daughter of St. Stephen of Hungary. Margaret was charming, intelligent, cultured, and lovely. She grew up at the court in Hungary that was sophisticated and surrounded by beauty.

When Margaret was about ten, her father's uncle, St. Edward the Confessor, became King of England, and it was safe for them to return from exile. Her father died shortly after their return, but Margaret was brought up at the court of King Edward the Confessor, the Saint.

Margaret was a devout youth and the example of the king was not lost on her. She read widely, especially the works of St. Augustine. It was said that she became the most learned woman in the land in her times.

When King Edward died, Margaret's brother, Edgar, was in line for the throne.

But William the Conqueror invaded England and defeated the English at the Battle of Hastings in 1066. Edgar and his family fled by sea. A violent storm wrecked their ship off the coast of Scotland.

They were rescued and taken to the court of King Malcolm. It was very primitive, a rough hunting lodge; the people were crude. It was a life in the wilds. Then the king fell in love with Margaret and asked her to be his queen. She had wanted to retire to a convent, but duty told her she must accept. Scotland was blessed. She used her power to bring faith and learning to these unlettered people.

The Church was isolated there and tribes were constantly fighting with one another. Queen Margaret promoted the love of God and lifted up her people in every way. She was the Mother of Scotland.

King Malcolm had a hot temper and was not a holy man, yet he loved Margaret and saw that she was greatly helping his people. They had six boys and two girls, and she raised them up to be God-fearing and righteous. Three of her sons became kings as well as two of her grandchildren and two great grandchildren. Historians say they were the best kings Scotland ever had. It shows what one good woman can do.

While Margaret raised good children, she also greatly influenced the nation. She saw that orphans were cared for, ransomed slaves, helped the poor, and righted the injustices of people treated unfairly. She was a mother to all.

## Prayer

DEAR St. Margaret, queen and mother and helper of the poor, pray that mothers today may follow your example and teach their children about Jesus. It is never easy to be a mother and especially in troubled times like ours.

So many influences seek to undermine the family. Peer pressure is great for youth to think mothers are old-fashioned and ignore their words. Help our mothers to persevere, and enable our teens to see that mothers are wise. Amen.

## 20th Day
## ST. ANTHONY OF EGYPT
**Founder of Monasticism**

c.251-c.354                                      Feast: January 17

THE Desert Fathers can give us a very important perspective on Christianity. Since the world would not accept the principles of Christ, they left the world. The world continued to prefer the darkness to the light. They went to the desert to escape the paganism of the world. St. Anthony was one of the first hermits.

Anthony was the son of a wealthy Egyptian. He worked on his father's prosperous farm along the Nile. He was a youth of strong build, bronze skin, high cheekbones, and big dark eyes. The father imparted his piety to his son.

For Anthony, Christ gave us a way of life that could not be questioned. He prayed often. At his father's bidding, he kept away from the Greeks in Egypt and their schools whose teachings ended in skepticism. But he read the Bible faithfully.

When Anthony was twenty, his parents died. He had always been an obedient son. Now the farm belonged to him and he was a prosperous farmer. But he who had always obeyed his earthly father now wished to obey more closely his heavenly Father.

Anthony heard the priest read the Gospel about the young man who asked Jesus what he must do to gain eternal life. Jesus told him to sell everything and follow Him.

After Mass, Anthony sold his farm and gave the money to the poor. He decided on a complete break with his former life. There was a holy old man who had fled the persecutions and now lived by himself in prayer and sacrifice. From him Anthony learned a way to live close to Christ.

Anthony went into the wilderness. He sought solitude so that he could pray and do penance and live for Jesus alone. He left the world and lived in a cave. But he soon found that the world had not left him. Tormented by many temptations, he prayed all the more and overcame them. He fasted and did penance. Admitting his weakness, he pleaded for God to help him.

Anthony became a holy man. He counseled the doubtful and sinners who sought him out. Anthony's withdrawal from the world inspired the monastic movement of later centuries. His example of holiness sowed the seed that sprouted up and produced much fruit. He taught all Christians that one must have silence for prayer. Silence teaches us how to speak to God, and when we speak to Him, He comes to us.

### Prayer

**D**EAR St. Anthony, you taught us the great importance of prayer. Nothing we do is more vital. Never let us neglect prayer. Obtain for us a love of prayer.

Enable us to realize that we cannot survive without God's grace, and one of the best ways to obtain it is through fervent prayer. Help us to persevere in prayer to gain the assistance we need in the trials and tribulations of life. Amen.

## 21st Day
## ST. JOAN OF ARC
### The Maid of Orleans

1412-1431                    Feast: May 30

JOAN saved France from its enemies, although she was a young unlearned girl. She was a simple peasant girl like many others. But then she began to hear voices that told her to go to the aid of her country. Orleans was under siege; the Dauphin, the future king of France, had fled from the north of France, and the victorious English were tracking him down.

**67**

Joan's shining, vital temperament, ever spontaneous and simple, responded to this call. She persuaded a relative to take her to see the Captain of the garrison, Robert de Baudricourt, so she could ask him to escort her to the Dauphin. St. Michael, she said, told her to do this. It was truly brave, for Joan was a peasant youth who didn't even know how to ride a horse.

Joan spoke to Sir Robert and told him that the Dauphin would be crowned king despite all his enemies. Robert asked her who told her this. Joan said simply, "The King of Heaven." The Captain was shocked. He couldn't believe her and sent her home.

Joan, however, was not discouraged. Later she again approached Baudricourt. This time he listened, because the French forces continued to be badly beaten. Joan was escorted to the Dauphin. The Dauphin, Charles, tested her, slipping in among the many people in the hall and putting another on the throne. But when she entered, she went up to him at once.

Charles still was doubtful, but then Joan told him exactly what he had said to God when he prayed alone, and he believed. As she requested, he gave her armor and the command of troops. Under her banner, she set out to rescue Orleans from the English.

At first the French commander would not obey her. But things got worse, and he gave in. Under her leadership the French broke the siege.

Joan told Charles he must be crowned king in the Cathedral in Reims, the traditional place of coronations. It was, however, still in enemy territory and Charles was fearful. Courageously, Joan and her troops escorted the Dauphin through the dangerous area. The English attacked, but her forces defeated them in several battles.

Joan entered Reims in triumph. She stood beside Charles as he was crowned king in the great Cathedral.

Joan went on to try to free Paris but was wounded and captured. She was tried by the English as a witch and burned at the stake at the age of nineteen. But the Church declared her a Saint.

### Prayer

DEAR St. Joan, you did what God willed no matter how difficult it was. Teach us to do God's will. Ask Jesus to grant us His light so that we may know His way for us and His grace so that we may follow it.

Help us to thank God for countless past blessings and always put our trust in Him. For without God we can do nothing. Amen.

# 22nd Day

# ST. BRENDAN

### Missionary to the New World

483-577                              Feast: May 16

WHEN St. Augustine was dying in Carthage, and the North African city was suffering terribly under siege by the barbarians, he told the people to have faith in God, Who would bring light to the darkness somehow. And so He did. As darkness descended on Africa, St. Patrick was on the way to Ireland to convert the people there, one of the greatest jewels in the crown of Catholicism. And one of the brightest of the Irish gems was Brendan.

The bishop, Erc, had told Brendan's mother that she would bear a son, great in power and rich in grace. And St. Becc Mac De prophesied, "There shall be born this night a true and worthy person whom kings and princes will honor, and whom he shall guide to heaven." That night the baby Brendan was born in the district of Tralee.

Patrick, heroic missionary, Patron of the Emerald Isle, brought the Faith to this country, and numerous brave young men turned from war to Christ, courageously serving at tremendous sacrifice Someone worth serving.

Brendan became a monk. He lived most of the day in silence. He said, "Two-thirds of piety consists of silence." It is in silence that one can pray. And prayer is the key to sanctity.

One day Brendan met a funeral procession. A young man had died. Filled with sorrow, Brendan told the weeping relatives to have faith and pray. The incredible happened. The dead youth was restored to life.

In time Brendan became the leader of a large monastery. He himself was astonished at all the young men who came to join them.

Later Brendan sought more solitude. He went to sea in a small ship, seeking to find an isolated island where he could pray in peace all day. He set sail in the mist to the west. Some say, going west from Ireland, shrinking from no peril, he crossed the ocean and found Newfoundland. Legend has it that he was the first European to discover the New World.

At length Brendan returned home. He was greatly honored for his discoveries and his difficult struggles against the raging sea.

It was the year 577, a Sunday, May 16, and the holy man celebrated Mass and then announced his end was near. He died that day.

### Prayer

D EAR St. Brendan, you traveled far to bring Christ to others. Strengthen us to help others know about Jesus. We are His apostles today. He wants us to accept the Good News with all our hearts and "shout it from the housetops."

Do not let us be timid or mediocre Christ-followers. His last command was to go out and tell everyone about Him. Help us to do as He wishes. Amen.

# 23rd Day

# ST. JOHN FISHER

## Scholar, Bishop, and Martyr

1459-1535                                    Feast: June 22

HENRY VIII made himself the Pope in England. He was like a spoiled child. He didn't want anyone telling him what to do. He had many temper tantrums, like a little kid in his terrible two's. So when he wanted a divorce and the Pope would not give it to him, he divorced himself from the Catholic Church. As the Pope for the Church of England, the first thing he did was to divorce his lawful wife. Very convenient! And woe to anyone in his kingdom who disagreed with this proud, pompous, little-minded man.

Most of the bishops were weak, subservient political appointments, and they bowed to this wish of Henry. But one bishop, John Fisher, did not. He was the most intelligent of them all. He would honor Henry as his king, but his conscience would not let Henry be his Pope.

John knew the stubborn, selfish King would seek revenge. A person who contradicted Henry most often was killed.

Though a bishop in an age of glitter for the hierarchy, John Fisher lived in poverty. He was a man of prayer and penance. He took seriously his role as shepherd. He was the servant of Christ and of the people.

John Fisher was tall and thin, white-haired, and had eyes that seemed to see beyond this world. Soon Henry, in a fit of temper, had this renegade bishop arrested. What a contrast between king and bishop—the king: carnal, crude and fat; and the Bishop of Rochester: an ascetic, an intellectual, the only one who remained loyal to Christ, which, to Henry, was disloyalty to him.

John Fisher was fixed in mind and heart on Jesus. This cannot be said of the passionate king and his vulgar court.

Bishop John was thrown into a dungeon in the Tower of London and left to rot for a year. Then he was put to death. The day was June 22, 1535. Bishop John on that day was awakened from sleep and told he was to die. He got up calmly and began to pray. He was very weak and sick from the cruel punishment of many months in the dungeon.

He said, "I thank the Lord for this day, and I trust in His mercy and goodness."

And he went out to his execution.

### Prayer

BISHOP John, you are a model for today. These days many are telling us to change the teachings of Christ and make them easier. You stood up for the truth. You knew that no human can add to or take away from the teachings Jesus gave us. You had such great faith in this that you gave your life for Jesus.

Let us not be misled, St. John. You were highly intelligent; help us not to be fooled by the half-educated who with high-sounding words want to change the priceless, precious message of Jesus. Amen.

## 24th Day
# ST. BENEDICT JOSEPH LABRE

**The Mendicant Pilgrim**

1748-1783                                    Feast: April 16

BENEDICT Joseph was poor. He died
in Rome as a beggar. Within a year
his reputation for sanctity was wide-
pread. As Cardinal John Wright said, "The
Saints always belong to the present." They
are truly diverse, and yet they are our own
brothers and sisters in Christ.

Benedict Joseph, from the beginning, did
not see the things of the world as impor-

tant. His eyes were not fixed on possessions but on Christ. This world was passing; he longed only to be with Christ in heaven. He could not understand how people contended for money and buying things, thinking this made them important. How childish! And people with childish minds could not understand him.

With the wisdom that comes from fervent prayer, the Saint knew that only one thing and one thing alone was important—Jesus.

Benedict Joseph was a quiet, meditative individual. Because he was thoughtful, he saw at once that the things of this life are worthless compared to walking with Jesus.

When Benedict Joseph was eighteen, an epidemic fell upon the city. He did not hesitate, but, as others were fleeing, he went to help the unfortunate sick and dying. He busied himself helping them.

Benedict Joseph had no home, but this never worried him. He slept where he could. Nothing seemed to trouble the youth. He knew God would take care of him.

In time he applied to a number of monasteries, but all refused him. He decided to live for Christ in poverty in the world. It was hard and lonely. He was a beggar and an outcast, wandering about like a tramp with old clothes and battered shoes.

The Saint ate whatever people gave him. If they gave him more than his simple diet, he would give it to others. He prayed as he walked along, praising God for sunshine, rain, and snow.

Benedict Joseph represents a Western example of the Eastern ascetical vocation of the mendicant pilgrim or wandering holy man—"the fool of Christ." He could not think of worldly needs; his eyes were always lifted up to God.

His last year he spent in Rome. People thought he was peculiar. But when he died, the poor whom he helped cried, "The Saint is dead, the Saint is dead."

### Prayer

DEAR St. Benedict Joseph, you showed us that the things of this world are nothing compared to the things of God. We are constantly being told by advertising that we can buy happiness. But it is not for sale.

Jesus is Joy. The trouble with many possessions is that we do not possess them— they possess us. Help us to see this as you did. Amen.

# 25th Day

# ST. ELIZABETH OF PORTUGAL

## Model Queen and Peacemaker

1271-1336                                      Feast: July 4

ELIZABETH'S father was a prince, successor to the King of Aragon in Spain. He was not a good man but was wise enough to know that, as he said, "the country people are those God loves more than the nobles and knights."

Elizabeth grew up at court, which was hardly a model nursery for a Saint. In time her father became King Pedro III. Elizabeth was a royal princess, charming, sweet, and delightful. Her father said she was his angel. She had wisdom and good sense. She prayed devoutly and read pious books. King Pedro said his daughter's prayers brought happiness to his kingdom.

Princess Elizabeth was given in marriage to the King of Portugal and so became the queen of that land. Now she brought happiness to Portugal. By prayer, and supplication to the Pope, she was able to get the Holy Father to lift the excommunication from her husband, King Diniz, and the interdict from Portugal, for past misdeeds.

Elizabeth was known to the people, especially the peasants who suffer most in war, as the Patroness of Peace. To ward off a civil war in Portugal between her husband and his brother, the queen summoned a peace conference and the conflict was averted.

The reign of King Diniz, largely because of Queen Elizabeth, was called the golden age of Portugal. Farming prospered, and she founded the first agricultural college.

Unfortunately the king, like most kings, had love affairs with various women at court. During these trying times Elizabeth found peace in prayer.

The Queen was most generous in almsgiving. She also went to a conference with Queen Maria in Spain and the two queens brought about a peace settlement.

Everyone knew of Elizabeth's kindness. And as the king lived loosely, so much the more did she do penance for him. Her noble heart went out to all. She constantly gave to the poor.

Queen Elizabeth knew many trials, including being exiled from the court, and the humiliation of being placed in charge of the king's illegitimate children. But her heart was full of love for these youngsters and she took them in as her own.

In all her difficulties, she prayed and had peace of soul.

## Prayer

YOU were noble in many ways, dear St. Elizabeth, but most of all you were a woman of goodness in loving your family and teaching them about Jesus. What could be more important in the world? In our short lives, we can spend our time either thinking of ourselves and our pleasures or, like the Saints, helping others, and especially the children who are so often neglected.

There are today among the young many religious illiterates. Pray that we may have good mothers to teach Christ to their children. Amen.

# 26th Day

## ST. MALACHY

### Reformer of Irish Catholicism

1095-1148                              Feast: November 3

S T. Malachy was born and lived in County Down. In that area was the village of Saul, where St. Patrick had offered his first and last Mass in Ireland; and there was Downpatrick, where lay the bodies of Patrick, St. Brigid, and St. Columcille. Danish invasions with horrible burning and plundering took place there. But when Malachy was born, there was peace.

His father, a nobleman, was a scholar. He died when the lad was seven. Malachy, too, was gifted in mind. He treasured learning, and he loved long walks. He prayed as he went along.

In time the young man became a priest, known for being devoted to the poor—all gentleness and mercy. He himself lived in poverty. Then he was appointed Abbot of Bangor, known for its holiness. Next he became the Bishop at Down and Connor (Antrim). He was only thirty years old.

Soon after, Malachy became the Archbishop of Armagh, the foremost See in all of Ireland. He knew it was a difficult assignment, and said to the one giving him his appointment, "You are leading me to death, but I obey hoping for martyrdom."

As the Saint grew older, he resigned from Armagh and returned as Bishop to Down. He set his face on death. But when told to do so, he made the long and arduous journey to Rome to settle ecclesiastical affairs in Ireland. Kneeling at the feet of Pope Innocent II, he humbly begged his blessings for his homeland. The Holy Father was so pleased with Bishop Malachy that he took his miter from his own head and placed it on the head of the Irishman.

Returning home, the Saint founded a Trappist monastery at Mellifont. In France, he had met the great Saint and reformer, St. Bernard of Clairvaux, and admired greatly his Cistercian monastery.

All his life Malachy lived without personal possessions. If he had been allowed, he would have became a Trappist monk himself. When the first Trappist Pope, Eugene III, asked his old abbot St. Bernard for guidance, the Saint said, "Study the life and follow the example of Malachy, and all will be well."

The truth of the Faith was always most dear to Malachy. He often secretly and with great compassion talked to a wayward brother-priest, seeking to bring him back to Jesus.

## Prayer

D EAR St. Malachy, you were an out-standing priest. Intercede with Jesus to bless us with good priests—those who will remain close to Him and realize that prayer must come first in their lives. Ask Jesus to teach our priests that learning is good and so is action, but prayer is most important. Let them see that they are but instruments of the Lord, through whose prayers graces flow to the people.

St. Malachy, pray that God will send us prayerful priests. Amen.

# ST. FRANCIS BORGIA

## Model Parent and Religious

1510-1572                    Feast: October 10

**F**RANCIS ran contrary to the Borgia tradition and became a Saint. He was born in a palace and received the education of a young Spanish grandee. He liked sports, and was a good student, and excelled in music. Some hymns he composed are sung in Spain today.

At seventeen, Francis was sent to the court of King Charles V at Valladolid. Enroute he saw a man with a limp being led by guards to the prison of the Inquisition. It was Ignatius Loyola, founder of the Jesuits that Francis would eventually join.

At court this tall, handsome youth became a favorite of Emperor Charles. And soon he fell in love with Eleanor de Castro, first lady in waiting of the empress. They were married and were happy and had eight children.

Then Empress Isabella died. Francis accompanied the coffin to Grenada, where she was to be buried. As an officer of the court, he had to officially identify the body at Granada. The coffin was opened and the body was already corrupting. The shock of this sight always remained with him—this beautiful, powerful woman decaying.

Francis was appointed Viceroy of Catalonia, and he and Eleanor and their children moved to Barcelona. Conditions were so bad that robbers overran the whole area. Political corruption was rampant. Francis at once started a vigorous campaign of reform. The poor loved him for making the streets and highways safe again. He was always gracious to the needy, giving them food and clothing out of his own funds.

When his father died, Francis was recalled to his home to be the Duke of Gandia and Marquis of Lombay. Three years later Eleanor died. He was consoled by a devout priest, a member of the new Jesuit Order. Francis later joined the Jesuits, after providing for his family.

Francis first engaged in parish work in the wilds of Northern Spain. Then he went on a series of journeys for Ignatius and next was treasurer of the Jesuits for Spain. He went all over the country building colleges, settling disputes, and establishing parishes.

In 1565 Francis was elected the Superior General of the Jesuits. He founded numerous colleges and sent missionaries all over the world.

### Prayer

ST. Francis, help us. You lived in difficult times. So do we. Many today are only seeking pleasure, then they wonder why they feel empty. So then, without Christ, they end up in pessimism and despair.

Help people to know that happiness comes from God. Prayer brings peace of soul. Those running around looking for fun end up unhappy and miserable. Save them from a wretched life. Amen.

# 28th Day

## ST. LOUIS

### A Truly Christian King

1214-1270                    Feast: August 25

L OUIS was King of France and an outstanding monarch, showing justice to all, promoting education, and helping the poor.

King Louis IX was a member of the Third Order of St. Francis. Once he made a visit to Brother Giles, one of St. Francis' first companions. The old friar knelt before the young king, and the young king also knelt to the holy Brother. They put their arms around one another. Neither said a word, but they parted dear friends.

King Louis liked counselors who said what they thought, and he distrusted those who always tried to flatter him or always agreed with him.

He became king at the age of twelve. His mother, the queen-dowager, was regent during his younger years. Queen Blanche brought him up in the Faith. She said, "I would rather see you dead at my feet than to commit one mortal sin."

The barons of France, having a woman and a boy to deal with, soon started trouble. Some began a rebellion, but Paris rose to the defense of the boy-king and his mother, and the insurrection was put down.

As king, Louis was dedicated to fairness for all. Later, he told his oldest son, "I pray you to make yourself beloved by the people." His own popularity rested on his concern for all the people, high and low. His days, he felt, were not his own but belonged to the people of France.

A reasonable and moderate man, Louis never failed to pray. Another said, "King Louis was considered by far the wisest of his advisers."

After Mass each morning he went outside and, under a tree, heard and settled the complaints and problems of all who came to him. He was truly a Christian king.

The story is told that one day a servant came rushing in to the king as he sat reading, "Come quickly, your Majesty," she said. "Christ has appeared above the altar in the chapel." The king replied, "I know well that Christ is in the chapel in the Eucharist," and went on reading.

Louis knew great suffering. He went on a crusade, and it was a total failure. He was taken prisoner and was released only after a large ransom was paid for him. Later, he embarked on a second crusade but died in

North Africa when a plague broke out in his army.

## Prayer

GOOD and worthy King Louis, help our leaders to be just in all things as you were. Pray that God will give them wisdom, so that they may direct the affairs of state with knowledge and understanding. Obtain for them courage, so that they can resist the temptation to be popular or make money, but, rather, dedicate themselves to serving the people.

The problems in our nation and in the world are many. We need divine light and divine help. Assist us, dear St. Louis. Amen.

# 29th Day

## ST. OLIVER PLUNKET

**Restorer of the Irish Church**

1629-1681                                    Feast: July 11

IRELAND was in agony. England had conquered the little island. There were years of warfare and bloodshed, and finally Cromwell crushed the Irish.

During these terrible years Oliver came on the scene. He was educated by an uncle, Bishop of Armagh and Meath. He was a good student and a spiritual boy. He wanted to be a priest and was sent to Rome to study at the Irish College.

Oliver compiled a brilliant academic record and was ordained. Ordinarily, he would have returned to Ireland, but Cromwell was trying to destroy the little country, so the new priest was assigned to teach in Rome at a college for missionaries. He spent many hours in prayer, preparing himself for the ordeal that lay ahead.

The news from Ireland was bad. The bloody English persecution continued. Three Irish bishops were killed, the others sent into exile. There were only two left in Ireland, one very old, the other in hiding. The English mistakenly thought they had crushed the Catholic Church.

The foremost See in Ireland, since the days of Patrick, was Armagh. Many candidates were proposed, but Pope Clement said, "Why should we look elsewhere when the best choice is right here in Rome?"

Oliver Plunket returned to his homeland as Archbishop of Armagh. He worked endlessly, comforting the people and strengthening their faith. He had to travel in disguise with priest-hunters on his trail. He slept on straw and had little food. Oliver lived in the wilds and was tormented by physical ailments, but the Archbishop made his rounds in fair weather and foul.

Years passed. Then there was a new eruption of anti-Catholic feeling among the English overlords.

Oliver was captured and put in prison. He lingered there for many months. A trial was held, and he was accused of treason. But he was acquitted. However, Lord Shaftesbury, a powerful London bigot, insisted he be brought to England. There he was locked up in the notorious Newgate prison with rats and filth and every disease.

When Oliver was taken to court, the judge said there had been no trial in Ireland. Oliver was tried again and found guilty of spying, because as in the trial of

Christ witnesses were paid to tell lies about him. He was hanged.

### Prayer

DEAR St. Oliver Plunket, you knew much suffering in life. You also knew that prayer is our salvation. Help us to be inspired by your heavenly wisdom. Too many today follow purely human wisdom, which leads into the swamp.

Teach us to put our trust and hope in God, pray faithfully, and be patient with God. He certainly is patient with us. Enable us to look to the Lord, as you did in all things. Amen.

## 30th Day
# ST. BERNARD OF CLAIRVAUX
### Reformer of the Cistercian Order

1090-1153                    Feast: August 20

S T. Bernard was the Abbot of the Trappist monastery at Clairvaux in France. Under his guidance, it was a model of strict observance. He decried the disciplinary decline in other monasteries and reformed many of them. This caused great controversies. Though he only wanted to be a monk who prayed, most of his life he found himself in the center of a great storm.

Changing people for the better is never popular. Bernard even wrote to Cardinals, kings, and Popes and told them they were doing wrong. But the people saw his goodness, and many of the young came to follow him. In all, he founded sixty-eight new monasteries.

Bernard was a very spiritual man, plunged deeply into the mysteries of Christ. With a heart on fire, he was an ardent apostle in a time of apathy and mediocrity.

Bernard was at once a contemplative and a great man of action. He did not relish being in the world; he wanted to pray. Always he feared being defiled by the world. But he knew he must do God's will and strike out strongly against the many evils of the day.

He said, "Because in the home to which we are journeying there are many mansions, therefore we do not all take one road. But we shall each be careful to make sure that the road we take does not lead us away from our goal."

He wrote, "Woe to us if we merely shine! When we shine, human beings honor us. But to me the judgment of humans is a small matter. It is the Lord Who judges me, and what He expects from all of us is not radiant brilliancy but fiery heat."

The Saint said in a sermon, "I do not say that we ought to neglect material things, or that by neglecting them we become spiritual. We must pray. We succeed spiritually by saving grace."

Bernard told people it is necessary that they know where they are going in life. The great goal of the Christian is heaven, to be with God and be happy forever.

To gain this goal, believers must know Christ and Him crucified. They must embrace Jesus and follow His ways; that is, love Him. His love for us puts us to shame. Pray that His love will fill your heart.

When we begin to understand how generously we are loved, we love Jesus more.

### Prayer

DEAR St. Bernard, you were a man of great prayer. Help us to pray more fervently and to thank God more faithfully. Let us give Him thanks for sending His Son to us. We would be lost without Him. Obtain for us the wisdom to pray daily as you did, from our hearts.

May we thank God for all His gifts in life: family, friends, the holy Church to guide us. Pray that God will bless our loved ones every day, and bless all those in need in the world. Amen.